Body Coverings

Skin

Cassie Mayer

Heinemann
LIBRARY

H **www.heinemann.co.uk/library**
Visit our website to find out more information about **Heinemann Library** books.

To order:
☎ Phone 44 (0) 1865 888066
📄 Send a fax to 44 (0) 1865 314091
💻 Visit the Heinemann Bookshop at www.heinemann.co.uk/library to browse our catalogue and order online.

First published in Great Britain by Heinemann Library, Halley Court, Jordan Hill, Oxford OX2 8EJ, part of Harcourt Education. Heinemann is a registered trademark of Harcourt Education Ltd.

Editorial: Tracey Crawford, Cassie Mayer, Dan Nunn, and Sarah Chappelow
Design: Jo Hinton-Malivoire
Picture Research: Tracy Cummins
Production: Duncan Gilbert

Originated by Chroma Graphics (Overseas) Pte. Ltd
Printed and bound in China by South China Printing Company

13 digit ISBN 978 0 431 18282 7 (hardback)

11 10 09 08 07 06
10 9 8 7 6 5 4 3 2 1

13 digit ISBN 978 0 431 18288 9 (paperback)

11 10 09 08 07
10 9 8 7 6 5 4 3 2 1

British Library Cataloguing in Publication Data
Mayer, Cassie
 Skin. – (Body coverings)
 1.Skin – Juvenile literature
 I.Title
 591.4'7

Acknowledgements
The publishers would like to thank the following for permission to reproduce photographs:
Corbis pp. **7** and **8** (Lynda Richardson), **12** (Ralph A. Clevenger), **13** and **14** (Daniel J. Cox), **15** and **16** (Joe McDonald), **20** (Kevin Dodge), **23** (scales and snake, Joe McDonald), **23** (manatee, Daniel J. Cox); FLPA pp. **11** and **12** (Minden Pictures), **22** (iguana); Getty Images pp. **6** (Balfour), **9** and **10** (Parfitt), **17** and **18** (Wolfe); Getty Images/Digital Vision pp. **4** (kingfisher and leopard), **5**, **22** (hippo), **23**; Getty Images/PhotoDisc p. **4** (snail and lizard); Science Photo Library p. **22** (sweat, Dick Luria).

Cover image of elephant skin reproduced with permission of Wyman/Getty Images. Back cover image of a frog reproced with permission of Wolfe/Getty Images.

Every effort has been made to contact copyright holders of any material reproduced in this book. Any omissions will be rectified in subsequent printings if notice is given to the publishers.

The paper used to print this book comes from sustainable resources.

Contents

feathers

shell

scales

fur

All animals have body coverings.
Look at these body coverings.

skin

Some animals have skin.
Skin is a body covering too.

There are different types of skin.

Skin can be wet.
What animal is this?

This animal is a salamander.
It breathes through its wet skin.

Skin can be dry.
What animal is this?

This animal is an elephant.
Its skin has wrinkles.

Skin can be smooth.
What animal is this?

This animal is a dolphin.
Its smooth skin helps it swim fast.

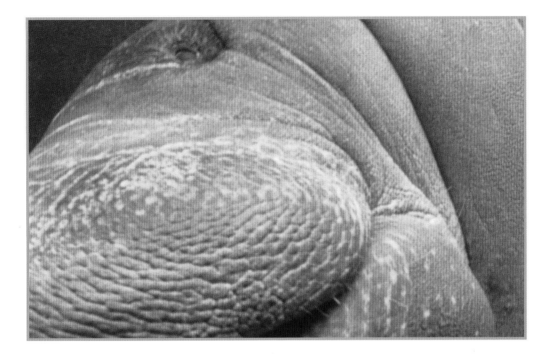

Skin can be rough.
What animal is this?

This animal is a manatee.
Its skin is very tough.

Skin can be scaly.
What animal is this?

This animal is a snake.
It sheds its skin.

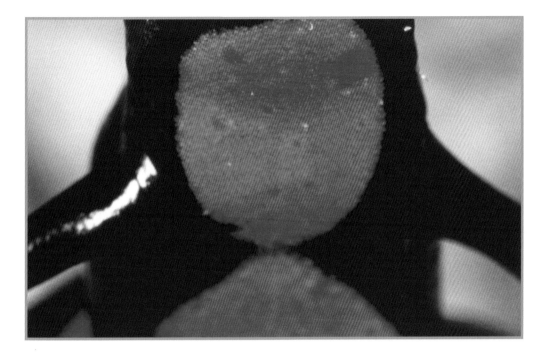

Skin can be bright colours.
What animal is this?

This animal is a poison dart frog.
Its skin says "Danger!".

Do you have skin?

Yes! You have skin!

Skin quiz

(answers on page 24)

1. I am very big.
    My skin has wrinkles.
    I have a long trunk.
    What am I?

2. I live in the sea.
    My skin is smooth.
    My smooth skin helps me swim fast.
    What am I?

Fun skin facts

Humans and other animals sweat through their skin. Sweating keeps them cool.

Iguanas have skin that stops their body from drying out.

Hippos have a built-in sunscreen. Their body makes a liquid that protects their skin.

Picture glossary

scaly covered in scales

shed to cast off an old skin

skin a type of body covering

waterproof not changed by water

Index

Notes to parents and teachers

Before reading

Talk about how animals have different body coverings – fur, feathers, shells, scales, and skin. Talk about the different kinds of skin – some skin is smooth (worm), some skin is rough (toad), some skin is wet (frog), and some skin is dry and scaly (lizard). Talk about the skin on our bodies. Ask the children if it feels wet or dry. Does it stretch? Explain that we don t shed our skin all in one go like a snake but we lose the outer layer of skin all the time.

After reading

Collect pictures of children with different skin colours from magazines Talk about the wide range of skin colours people have. Collect pictures of different animals e.g. snakes, dolphins, elephants, lizards. Ask the children to sort them into categories e.g. wet, smooth, dry, rough. Prepare two bowls: one of cold water and one of warm water. Ask children to put their hand in one of the bowls of water. Hold it there for 10 seconds. Then ask their friend to feel the hand. Does it feel hot or cold?

Answers to quiz: 1. I am an elephant. 2. I am a dolphin.